PAMPHLETS ON AMERICAN WRITERS · NUMBER 19

UNIVERSITY OF MINNESOTA

⤾ *Benjamin Franklin*

BY THEODORE HORNBERGER

UNIVERSITY OF MINNESOTA PRESS · MINNEAPOLIS

BENJAMIN FRANKLIN

THEODORE HORNBERGER, a professor of English at the University of Pennsylvania, is co-editor of the two-volume work *The Literature of the United States* and the author of a number of other books.

⤳ *Benjamin*
Franklin

Nothing goes by luck in composition," Thoreau remarked in his journal in 1841. "It allows of no tricks. The best you can write will be the best you are. Every sentence is the result of a long probation. The author's character is read from title-page to end."

The Comte de Buffon is supposed to have meant much the same thing by his statement that the style is the man, and the concept is held in general esteem. It presents some difficulties, however, when applied to Benjamin Franklin, a man whose character remains mysterious and whose voluminous writings are full of what he himself regarded as tricks of his trade.

Many readers may indeed be surprised to find Franklin discussed in a series devoted to American authors. His fame rests less upon authorship than upon other things. Printer, scientist, statesman, and promoter of schools, libraries, hospitals, insurance companies, savings banks, and the post office, he would be conspicuous among American notables if he had never written a line.

Nevertheless, when in 1771 he began to compose his widely read autobiography, he put "My writing" at the head of the topics to be treated and proceeded to give careful attention to his experience in mastering English composition, which he thought had contributed greatly to his success in the various roles he had been called upon to play. He unquestionably fancied himself as a writer, and it is no more than fair to take him at his word.

Anyone who admires Franklin is likely to wish occasionally that he had written rather less than he did. Two pieces in particular —

and they happen to be his best known works — have provided much ammunition to his detractors and are likely to diminish his stature even among his friends.

The first is *The Way to Wealth*, originally the preface to *Poor Richard's Almanac* for 1758. It strung together into a connected narrative the pithy sayings relating to industry, frugality, and prudence from twenty-four earlier issues of Franklin's almanac, adding some new ones for good measure. Later separately published, *The Way to Wealth* is known in more than 150 editions, many of them translations into languages other than English. To its enormous audience Franklin and Poor Richard were indistinguishable, and hence arose the widespread impression that Franklin's basic faith was that "God helps them that help themselves" and his gospel that of acquisitiveness:

> Get what you can, and what you get hold;
> 'Tis the Stone that will turn all your lead into gold.

Those who think of Franklin as materialistic, cautious, and prudent to a fault can feel with some justice that like David Harum, the shrewd protagonist of Edward N. Westcott's novel of 1898, Franklin read the Golden Rule as "Do unto the other feller the way he'd like to do unto you an' do it fust."

One can argue that *The Way to Wealth* does not fairly represent either Poor Richard or his creator, but no such excuse can be offered for the worldliness of the *Autobiography*. In it Franklin candidly undertook to explain how he had risen in the world and his explanation is not a wholly pretty story. Advancement, he implied, is a matter of keeping an eye on the main chance. It requires calculation and may even mean using one's friends, flattering one's superiors, and suppressing one's opinions if they seem likely to offend influential people. The good life, according to the *Autobiography*, is not the pursuit of simple saintliness or spiritual serenity but the attainment of economic independence and social posi-

6

tion. The aura of finagling and of elasticity of conviction which surrounds the *Autobiography* offends many sensitive readers and is the justification for the castigation of Franklin by such critics as D. H. Lawrence. In his *Studies in Classic American Literature* Lawrence referred to Franklin as "snuff-coloured" and as wishing to confine the "dark vast forest" of the soul of man in a barbed-wire paddock, there to grow "potatoes or Chicagoes." The judgment is severe, but not a gross misrepresentation of Franklin as he explained himself in the *Autobiography*.

Neither his most popular writings nor his detractors, however, have utterly destroyed Franklin as a national hero. He was lionized during his lifetime and visitors still toss pennies on his grave in Christ Church Burying Ground in Philadelphia. How can this be, if his ideals were so pint-sized and mundane?

One answer is that the masses are always worldly in their aspirations and, since like appeals to like, commonplace people create commonplace heroes. Another is that the crowd is readily captured by showmanship, a quality which Franklin possessed as richly as any man of his time. A third answer, and perhaps the best one, is that no man really understands himself, Franklin not excepted. His practice did not always follow his precepts and he often acted upon rasher impulses and nobler principles than those which he publicly avowed. Many discrepancies between theory and practice can be demonstrated in his life and, as will appear, in his writing as well. He was not as uncomplicated a man as he thought he was, nor was his literary style as simple as he believed it to be.

His life can be quickly disposed of, since it is in its main outlines common knowledge.

The son of a candlemaker, he was born in Boston in 1706. After meager schooling he was apprenticed, at the age of twelve, to an older brother who was a printer. Five years later he ran away from home. Following some disillusioning adventures, including an eighteen-month residence in London, he settled in Philadelphia in 1726 and proceeded to make a modest fortune. By 1748 he was financially independent and freed himself from business to turn his abundant energy to science and public affairs. Within a few years he was internationally famous as the author of *Experiments and Observations on Electricity* (1751), a book which assured him a warm welcome when his political activities took him back to England in 1757. At this point the *Autobiography* ends.

Twenty-five of the remaining years of his life were spent in Europe. He was in London first (1757–62) as a representative of the Pennsylvania elected assembly and again (1764–75) as semiofficial ambassador of most of the British American colonies during the series of disputes about taxation which culminated in the Revolution. Finally (1776–85) he was in Paris, where he helped to secure desperately needed naval and military assistance for the armed struggle for independence and to negotiate the peace treaty which recognized the sovereignty of the United States. Suffering from a painful stone in the bladder, he returned at seventy-nine to Philadelphia, where he died in 1790, soon after taking part in the convention which drafted the Constitution. Of this long period of distinguished public service the *Autobiography* says almost nothing.

Europe first knew Franklin as a scientist, and remembered him as the man who rashly flew a kite in a thunderstorm to prove that lightning is an electrical phenomenon. To this dramatic picture others were added as his later life unfolded. One was that of the mild-mannered colonial agent, facing the House of Commons at the height of the Stamp Act crisis to answer 174 questions from friends and critics of the colonies with such directness as to astonish the House and enchant large sections of the British public. Another was of an old man in a fur cap and spectacles, who among the powdered wigs of Paris seemed the incarnation of the simple virtues of the New World, so that when he and Voltaire met at the Academy of Sciences the audience was not satisfied until the two *philosophes* hugged one another and exchanged kisses on both cheeks. Snuff-colored as his ideals may have been, the eighteenth century adored him. "He snatched the lightning from the sky and the sceptre from tyrants," Turgot the economist proclaimed in a famous epigram. He was more renowned, wrote his envious compatriot, John Adams, than Leibniz, Sir Isaac Newton, Frederick the Great, or Voltaire, and "more beloved and esteemed than any or all of them."

Franklin, then, was something more than "Poor Richard, the Boy Who Made Good," as Dixon Wecter labeled him in *The Hero in America*. The books on Franklin the "amazing" and the "many-sided" are not wholly in the wrong, nor are the biographers who have called him "the first civilized American," "the apostle of modern times," and, as Carl Van Doren happily phrased it, "a harmonious human multitude." For versatility, wide-ranging intellectual curiosity, and political acumen, Benjamin Franklin has had few peers. His *Autobiography* does him far less than justice.

With his writing as with his life one must begin with the *Autobiography*, but with the awareness that it does not tell the whole story. When he began to write it he was a man of sixty-five, generalizing about English composition as he was generalizing about worldly success, and interpreting his early experience in terms of maturity and mellowed memories.

By his own account Franklin was a precocious, bookish child, and his family naturally thought that he might become an ornament to the ministry, then the most honored profession in the Boston Puritan community. At eight, therefore, he was sent to Latin grammar school as a first step toward Harvard College and a Congregational pulpit. His father, however, thinking of the expense of a college education and the size of ministerial salaries, soon had a change of heart. After less than a year's exposure to Latin syntax he was withdrawn and enrolled in a private school which advertised, in the *Boston News-Letter*, instruction in "Writing, Cyphering, Treble Violin, Flute, Spinet, &c. Also English and French Quilting, Imbroidery, Florishing, Plain Work, Marking in several sorts of Stitches and several other works." In this evidently busy and co-educational establishment, he mastered penmanship but little else, failing, he recalled, in arithmetic. This took a year or so; at the age of ten his schooldays were over.

Home study was another matter. He could not remember when he learned to read, but at an early age was devouring what few books his father had accumulated. Among them were a number of works of theological controversy; he regretted later that more suitable material was not at hand when he was so eager for knowledge. He remembered three other books: Plutarch's *Lives*, Defoe's *Essay on Projects*, and Cotton Mather's *Essays to Do Good*. The time spent on Plutarch was not, he thought, wasted, and it may have had something to do with his lifelong taste for history and his delight in the delineation of character. From Defoe and Mather he derived, he said, a turn of thought which influenced some of the chief events of his later life, by which he no doubt meant his use of some of their ideas on education and mutual association for "good works." His first systematic purchases out of his spending money were works by John Bunyan. "Honest John," he wrote, "was the first that I know of who mix'd Narration & Dialogue, a Method of Writing very engaging to the Reader, who in the most interesting Parts finds himself as it were brought into the Company, & present at the Discourse. De foe in his Cruso, his Moll Flanders, Religious Courtship, Family Instructor, & other Pieces, has imitated it with Success. And Richardson has done the same in his Pamela, &c." Like Bunyan, Franklin was to make effective use of dialogue and allegory.

More books became available in his brother's print shop. The office stock was supplemented by loans from a friendly merchant. At night and early in the morning and whenever on Sunday he could get out of going to church, Franklin read and studied.

In 1718 he ventured into print with a topical ballad about a shipwreck, which sold well enough to make any twelve-year-old vain. Another on Blackbeard the pirate followed; then his father discouraged him "by ridiculing my Performances, and telling me Versemakers were always Beggars; so I escap'd being a Poet, most probably a very bad one." Thereafter he showed only a mild interest in poetry. He composed verses occasionally, but "approv'd the amusing one's Self with Poetry now & then, so far as to improve one's Language, but no farther."

The father's influence on his son's prose was rather happier. Among the boy's friends was another booklover, John Collins, with whom he was fond of arguing—a liking for argument, Franklin believed, had been one result of reading theological works. He and Collins debated the mental capacities of women and whether or not girls should be educated. Franklin, already on the side of the ladies, felt himself overpowered, not so much by Collins' logic as by his fluency. To present his own case effectively he wrote out his arguments in the form of letters and exchanged them with his friend. His father found this correspondence, made a point of discussing it, and observed that though Benjamin with his print-shop training had an advantage in spelling and punctuation he "fell far short in elegance of Expression, in Method and in Perspicuity, of which he convinc'd me by several Instances. I saw the Justice of his Remarks, & thence grew more attentive to the *Manner* in Writing, and determin'd to endeavour at Improvement." Franklin never deviated from his father's standards: elegance, in the sense of ingenious simplicity; method, or careful organization; and perspicuity, or complete clarity.

To improve his style Franklin adopted a device which other

would-be writers have found effective. He undertook to imitate the writing then most fashionable and admired, that of *The Spectator*. "I took some of the Papers," he tells us,

"& making short Hints of the Sentiment in each Sentence, laid them by a few Days, and then without looking at the Book, try'd to compleat the Papers again, by expressing each hinted Sentiment at length & as fully as it had been express'd before, in any suitable Words, that should come to hand.

"Then I compar'd my Spectator with the Original, discover'd some of my Faults & corrected them. But I found I wanted a Stock of Words or a Readiness in recollecting & using them, which I thought I should have acquir'd before that time, if I had gone on making Verses, since the continual Occasion for Words of the same Import but of different Length, to suit the Measure, or of different Sound for the Rhyme, would have laid me under a constant Necessity of searching for Variety, and also have tended to fix that Variety in my Mind, & make me Master of it. Therefore I took some of the Tales & turn'd them into Verse: And after a time, when I had pretty well forgotten the Prose, turn'd them back again. I also sometimes jumbled my Collections of Hints into Confusion, and after some Weeks, endeavour'd to reduce them into the best Order, before I began to form the full Sentences, & compleat the Paper. This was to teach me Method in the Arrangement of Thoughts. By comparing my work afterwards with the original, I discover'd many faults and amended them; but I sometimes had the Pleasure of Fancying that in certain Particulars of small Import, I had been lucky enough to improve the Method or the Language and this encourag'd me to think I might possibly in time come to be a tolerable English Writer, of which I was extreamly ambitious."

Those who cherish originality or believe in "inspiration" are sure to scorn Franklin's imitative methods. Fresh perception and wide reading are perhaps more valuable in the long run than laborious exercises such as his. On the other hand, there are few better ways of building a vocabulary and mastering the elements of logical organization. Compared to learning ten new words a day or outlining modern essays, Franklin's technique stands up well, and in his own case undoubtedly produced the results he sought.

To a modern eye the prose of Addison and Steele and the expository writing of Defoe seem overly contrived. They rely upon numerous parallelisms and contrasts, upon balance, antithesis, and climax. All good prose shows careful pruning, but eighteenth-century prose-writers, like eighteenth-century gardeners, were fond of the espalier method, patiently laboring to achieve a careful and instantly impressive structure rather than simply to cut out the dead wood and to increase the productiveness of the bearing branches. Some of Franklin's early prose was espaliered, but working against that tendency were other influences: his father's standards, the example of the Puritan sermon which he never mentions but to which he was exposed at an impressionable age, and his newspaper experience, which encouraged both conciseness and a conservatism about language.

His early fondness for contradiction, shared with his friend Collins, seemed to him later a bad habit. He claimed to have abandoned it after encountering the Socratic method of disputation, in which a point of view is established by a sequence of leading questions rather than by direct argument. His curiosity led him to Xenophon's *Memorabilia*; in emulation of Socrates he dropped "abrupt Contradiction, and positive Argumentation, and put on the humble Enquirer & Doubter." Finding the pose safe and successful, "I took a Delight in it, practis'd it continually & grew very artful & expert in drawing People even of superior Knowledge into Concessions the Consequences of which they did not foresee, entangling them in Difficulties out of which they could not extricate themselves, and so obtaining Victories that neither my self nor my Cause always deserved." This device, more useful in face-to-face oral discourse than in writing, became a part of his bag of tricks. As will appear, he often sought to assume the mask or persona of the humble inquirer and, keenly aware of the importance of his audience in determining his strategy, led his readers into unwary concessions.

As Franklin realized, the Socratic method contains an element of sophistry, in that there is some intentional deception. He said that he gradually gave it up, "retaining only the Habit of expressing my self in Terms of modest Diffidence, never using when I advance any thing that may possibly be disputed, the Words, *Certainly*, *undoubtedly*, or any others that give the Air of Positiveness to an Opinion; but rather say, *I conceive*, *or I apprehend* a Thing to be so and so, *It appears to me*, *or I should think it so and so for such & such Reasons*, or *I imagine* it to be so, or *it is so if I am not mistaken*. This Habit I believe has been of great Advantage to me, when I have had occasion to inculcate my Opinions & persuade Men into Measures that I have been from time to time engag'd in promoting. And as the chief Ends of Conversation are to *inform*, or to be *informed*, to *please* or to *persuade*, I wish wellmeaning sensible Men would not lessen their Power of doing Good by a Positive assuming Manner that seldom fails to disgust, tends to create Opposition, and to defeat every one of those Purposes for which Speech was given us, to wit, giving or receiving Information, or Pleasure." As a politician Franklin was remarkably faithful to this theory of oral discourse, of which the practicality is self-evident to anyone who has ever attended a public meeting or legislative assembly.

He also applied the strategy of the humble inquirer to writing. Good writing, he observed, "ought to have a tendency to benefit the reader, by improving his virtue or his knowledge. . . . an ill man may write an ill thing well; that is, having an ill design, he may use the properest style and arguments (considering who are to be readers) to attain his ends. In this sense, that is best wrote, which is best adapted for obtaining the end of the writer." He who would write to please good judges, Franklin said in 1733, should attend to three things: "That his Performance be *smooth*, *clear*, and *short*:

For the contrary Qualities are apt to offend, either the Ear, the Understanding, or the Patience." The audience, then, was always uppermost with Franklin the writer as well as the speaker.

His training and his theory, in short, gave Franklin some confidence in tricks. An examination of his writings will show how he used them and will also demonstrate, I hope, that he wrote with more variety, color, temper, and whimsey than he himself realized.

Aside from his ballads, neither of which has been certainly identified, Franklin's earliest literary efforts were the Silence Dogood papers, a series of fourteen essays printed in 1722 in the *New England Courant*, his brother's newspaper. The *Courant* had invited its readers to contribute suitable compositions. "I was excited," Franklin tells us, "to try my Hand among them. But being still a Boy, & suspecting that my Brother would object to printing any Thing of mine in his Paper if he knew it to be mine, I contriv'd to disguise my Hand, & writing an anonymous Paper I put it at Night under the Door of the Printing House." He was then sixteen.

The imitation of *The Spectator* is direct and immediate, as Elizabeth C. Cook has neatly shown. "I have observed," Addison began, "that a reader seldom peruses a book with pleasure till he knows whether the writer of it be a black or a fair man, of a mild or choleric disposition, married or a bachelor, with other particulars of the like nature, that conduce very much to the right understanding of an author." Franklin's second sentence was: "And since it is observed, that the Generality of People, now a days, are unwilling either to commend or dispraise what they read, until they are in some measure informed who or what the Author of it is, whether he be *poor* or *rich*, *old* or *young*, a *Scollar* or a *Leather Apron Man*, &c. and give their Opinion of the Performance, according to the Knowledge which they have of the Author's Circumstances, it may not be amiss to begin with a short Account of my past Life and present Condition, that the Reader may not be at a Loss to judge whether or no my Lucubrations are worth his reading." The idiom the boy so much admired is slightly localized by such invention as "Leather Apron Man," and conciseness is not yet a passion.

Franklin also shows himself a devotee of Addison and Steele in his persona and in his perception of his audience. Silence Dogood tells us that she was born en route from London to New England. "My Entrance into this troublesome World was attended with the Death of my Father, a Misfortune, which tho' I was not then capable of knowing, I shall never be able to forget; for as he, poor Man, stood upon the Deck rejoycing at my Birth, a merciless Wave entred the Ship, and in one Moment carry'd him beyond Reprieve. Thus was the *first* Day which I saw, the *last* that was seen by my Father; and thus was my disconsolate Mother at once made both a *Parent* and a *Widow*." (One can still feel the pride of the boy who polished off that last sentence, with its antithesis and ingeniously paradoxical climax.) Silence bears some resemblances to her creator. Her education was informal, picked up in the library of a bachelor country minister to whom she was bound at an early age, and who saw that she learned needlework, writing, and arithmetic before he at length married her. Their seven years of "conjugal Love and mutual Endearments" ended with his death, and left her with two likely girls, a boy, and her native common sense. She now enjoys the conversation of an honest neighbor, Rusticus, and an "ingenious" clergyman who boards with her, "and by whose Assistance I intend now and then to beautify my Writings with a Sentence or two in the learned Languages, which will not only be fashionable, and pleasing to those who do not understand it, but will likewise be very ornamental." (Franklin's flair for irony thus appears at the very beginning of his writing life.) Silence has, she admits, a "natural Inclination to observe and reprove the Faults of others," and in her third communication she reveals her calculation of her audience. "I am very sensible," she says, "that it is impossible for me, or indeed any *one* Writer to please *all* Readers at once. Various Persons have different Sentiments; and that which is pleasant and delightful to one, gives another a Disgust. He that would (in this Way of Writing) please all, is under a Necessity to make his Themes almost as numerous as his Letters. He must one while be merry and diverting, then more solid and serious; one while sharp and satyrical, then (to mollify that) be sober and religious; at *one* Time let the Subject be Politicks, then let the next Theme be Love. Thus will every one, one Time or another, find some thing agreeable to his own Fancy, and in his Turn be delighted."

For all his theory, Franklin was not yet a skillful writer. The Dogood papers lack plan, fail to sustain the point of view of the persona, and indeed permit that creation to fade gradually into limbo. Of the fourteen essays, the best are a dream allegory on education at Harvard College (No. 4) and a satire on the New England funeral elegy, with a hilarious recipe for writing one (No. 7). These two essays are the first revelation of Franklin the rebel, whose real feelings break through the mask. They attracted attention of a kind which in his more cautious moments Franklin sought to avoid. He gives as one of his reasons for leaving Boston "that I had already made myself a little obnoxious to the governing Party." The pose of the bland inquirer did not go well with satire.

Nor did the delight in logic and contradiction die as early a death as an unwary reading of the *Autobiography* may lead one to think. In 1725, working in Palmer's printing shop in London, Franklin helped set in type an edition of William Wollaston's *The Religion of Nature Delineated*. Finding himself questioning some of Wollaston's arguments, he wrote and had printed a brief, closely reasoned essay, the gist of which is that God is all-wise, all-good, and all-powerful, and that therefore neither evil nor free will actually exist. Whatever is, is right, Franklin asserted, and the principle which governs human behavior is not the ill-founded distinction between virtue and vice but the inexorable balancing out of pleasure and pain. In other words, *A Dissertation on Liberty and Necessity, Pleasure and Pain* reduces moral conduct to a matter of sound judgment, in which religious considerations are conspicuously absent. He tells us that his employer found the principles of his pamphlet "abominable," and he himself decided quickly that they were at the least injudicious. He destroyed most of the hundred copies that were printed and fifty years later told his friend Benjamin Vaughan that his views had changed.

The *Dissertation* is the only elaborate example of formal syllogistic reasoning among Franklin's works of persuasion. Its content and method go back to his early reading in theology, most probably to Samuel Clarke's Boyle Lecture sermons on the attributes of God (1704–5). That reading, said Franklin, "wrought an Effect on me quite contrary to what was intended by them: For the Arguments of the Deists which were quoted to be refuted, appeared to me much Stronger than the Refutations. In short I soon became a thorough Deist." A Deist he remained, writing to Ezra Stiles only five weeks before he died in terms parallel to those in the *Autobiography* and to the classic statement of Deistic principles in Lord Herbert of Cherbury's *De Veritate* (1624): "Here is my creed. I believe in one God, the creator of the universe. That he governs it by his Providence. That he ought to be worshipped. That the most acceptable service we render to him is doing good to his other children. That the soul of man is immortal, and will be treated with justice in another life respecting its conduct in this. These I take to be the fundamental points in all sound religion, and I regard them as you do in whatever sect I meet with them." Reason, not the Bible, was Franklin's standard for religious faith.

Franklin's exploration of the processes of persuasion was continued in two other early works: *A Modest Enquiry into the Na-*

ture and Necessity of a Paper-Currency (1729) and *Poor Richard's Almanac*, of which the first issue was that for 1733. Both were intimately connected with his main concern in the decade after his final settlement in Philadelphia in 1726 – to establish himself in his trade as a printer.

A Modest Enquiry appeared in the same year in which he acquired his newspaper, the *Pennsylvania Gazette*. His first venture into the realm of economic theory, it resembles neither the Addisonian essay nor the theological polemic, although it is a carefully structured argument. I suggest that its model was the Puritan sermon. No Biblical text heads it, to be sure, but in place of that authority is a truism to which no reader was likely to object: to carry on trade requires a "certain proportionate quantity of money . . . more than which would be of no advantage in trade, and less, if much less, exceedingly detrimental to it."

From this Franklin draws four axioms, roughly parallel to the "doctrines" which the Puritan preacher customarily derived from his text: (1) great scarcity of money means high interest rates; (2) great scarcity of money reduces prices; (3) great scarcity of money discourages the settlement of workmen and leads to the exodus of those already in the country; and (4) great scarcity of money, in such a country as America, leads to greater consumption of imported goods. Plentiful money of course produces exactly the opposite effects: low interest, good prices, encouragement of settlement and of home production.

What persons, he then asks, will be for or against the emission of a large additional amount of paper currency? Opposing it, he replies, in a passage with many emotional overtones, will be money-lenders, land speculators, lawyers, and the dependents of these classes. "On the other Hand, those who are Lovers of Trade, and delight to see Manufactures encouraged, will be for having a large Addition to our Currency." Furthermore, Franklin asserts, plenty of money will make land values rise, and will be to the advantage of England; a currency issue, therefore, will not be against the interest of either the proprietors (the Penn family) or the homeland.

He next turns to the question of whether or not the issue of more currency would lead to depreciation of its value. This demanded his consideration of the nature and value of money in general. To such theoretical discussion, in which he anticipates at some points Adam Smith's *The Wealth of Nations*, he devotes about half his entire space. A number of possible objections are then disposed of and the essay concludes with a paragraph in the persona of the humble inquirer, who had previously been conspicuously absent. "As this Essay is wrote and published in Haste, and the Subject in itself intricate, I hope I shall be censured with Candour, if, for want of Time carefully to revise what I have written, in some Places I should appear to have express'd my self too obscurely, and in others am liable to Objections I did not foresee."

Despite its final gesture of humility, *A Modest Enquiry* is basically an appeal to the self-interest of the masses, in which their prejudices against moneylenders, speculators, and lawyers were skillfully brought to bear upon a political issue. The piece was Franklin's first real success in persuasion. It was, he said, "well receiv'd by the common People in general; but the Rich Men dislik'd it; for it increas'd and strengthen'd the Clamour for more Money; and they happening to have no Writers among them that were able to answer it, their Opposition slacken'd, & the Point was carried by a Majority in the House. My Friends there, who conceiv'd I had been of some Service, thought fit to reward me, by employing me in printing the Money, a very profitable Jobb, and a great Help to me. This was another Advantage gain'd by my being able to write." The next year, one may add, he was appointed public printer of the province and his business success was thereafter never in doubt.

His decision to publish an almanac was natural for a young

printer. Almost everyone needed an almanac. It was a calendar, a record of historical anniversaries, a guide to the times of the rising and setting of the sun and of the phases of the moon. Farming and medical practice were still widely governed by folk belief in the influence of the heavenly bodies. Firewood, to burn well, had presumably to be cut while the moon was waxing, fruit gathered for the winter when it was on the wane. Horoscopes were cast to settle the proper moment to swallow medicine or wean babies. Moreover, since the aspect of the heavens varied with the latitude and longitude, it was not much use to have an almanac unless it was locally prepared. The almanac, consequently, had been a staple money-maker since the invention of printing and there were dozens in America, beginning with one for 1639 which is believed to have been the second imprint of the pioneer press at Cambridge.

In 1732 seven almanacs, one of them in German, were being printed in Philadelphia. The most successful was probably the *American Almanac*, begun by Daniel Leeds in 1686 and continued in Franklin's time by Leeds's son Titan. Despite this competition *Poor Richard's Almanac* was immediately successful. Three printings of the first issue were needed, and by the middle 1760's nearly 10,000 copies were being printed annually.

Franklin's triumph owed much to his creation of another persona: Richard Saunders, Philomath (i.e., astrologer). Richard confesses in his first preface that he is "excessive poor" and his wife "excessive proud." She cannot bear "to sit spinning in her Shift of Tow, while I do nothing but gaze at the Stars, and has threatned more than once to burn all my Books and Rattling-Traps (as she calls my Instruments) if I do not make some profitable Use of them for the Good of my Family. The Printer has offer'd me some considerable share of the Profits, and I have thus begun to comply with my Dame's Desire." The purchaser of his almanac, concludes Poor Richard, will get a useful utensil and also perform an act of charity.

A seventeenth-century English astrologer and almanac-maker had been named Richard Saunders and a popular eighteenth-century London almanac was called *Poor Robin's*. Poor Richard, nevertheless, is an imaginative although short-lived creation. At first he is an improvident and henpecked dreamer, not unlike Rip Van Winkle except for his interest in extracting pennies from the public. Within a few years he turns moralist, and in *The Way to Wealth* he is little more than a handy reference for the venerable Father Abraham, who inserts "as Poor Richard says" now and then to punctuate his sermon on the homely virtues. John F. Ross has suggested that like some later American comic creations Poor Richard gradually faded as his creator assumed the role of philosopher and oracle. The persona, in short, was neither developed nor long maintained.

The first few issues of Franklin's almanac are even more remarkable for his experiment with the hoax, a form of joke wherein he pushed the strategy of extracting unconscious concessions from an unsuspecting reader to its limit. A number of his finest pieces are hoaxes, presenting absurdities with such a poker-faced manner that even ordinarily perceptive readers were taken in. The classic example is his "Proposed New Version of the Bible," an ironic paraphrase of Job 1:6–11, which no less a reader than Matthew Arnold interpreted as a lapse of Franklin's customary good sense, failing to recognize it as an attack on the English king and his ministers.

The hoax which launched *Poor Richard's Almanac* was borrowed directly from Jonathan Swift, who in 1707–8 had attacked the pretensions of a London astrologer, John Partridge, in a series of papers purportedly written by Isaac Bickerstaff. Franklin adopted Swift's strategy and many of his details. Poor Richard asserts, in the preface which has been quoted, that he would have issued an almanac many years earlier had he not been "overpowered" by regard for Titan Leeds. This obstacle, he observes, is "soon to be removed, since inexorable Death, who was never known to respect Merit, has already prepared the mortal Dart, the fatal Sister has already extended her destroying Shears, and that ingenious Man must soon be taken from us." Leeds will die, predicts Poor Richard, on October 17, 1733. By Leeds's own calculation "he will survive till the 26th of the same Month. . . . Which of us is most exact, a little Time will now determine."

Leeds, like John Partridge, saw nothing funny in this macabre joke, and wrote the next year of the folly and ignorance of Poor Richard, who had not only lied about the date of his rival's death but had also perpetrated "another gross Falsehood in his said Almanack, viz. — *That by my own Calculation, I shall survive until the 26th of the said month* (October) which is as untrue as the former." To this Poor Richard replied, as Bickerstaff had to Partridge: "I convince him in his own Words, that he is dead . . . for in his Preface to his Almanack for 1734, he says, '*Saunders adds . . . that by my own Calculation I shall survive until the 26th of the said Month October 1733, which is as untrue as the former.*' Now if it be, as Leeds says, *untrue* and a *gross Falshood* that he surviv'd till the 26th of October 1733, then it is certainly *true* that he died *before* that Time . . . anything he may say to the contrary notwithstanding." In dealing with a satirist it is well to look to the precision of one's language.

Its opening gambit, however, it not what made *Poor Richard's Almanac* a continuing success. Its popularity grew along with Franklin's ingenuity in filling the spaces above, below, and beside his tables of dates and astronomical data with more readable material than his competitors could find. Little of it was original, but not much was borrowed without artful revision to make it more attractive to his audience. Perhaps the transformation of the dreamy astrologer into the moralist was determined by his largely rural audience, which honored hard work and saving more than jokes or sophisticated wit. At any rate, the "sayings" of Poor Richard eventually came close to being gospel to the country folk, and they still find a market in such little books as *Ben Franklin's Wit and Wisdom*.

Robert Newcomb, who has made the most extensive of the many studies of their origins, finds two major types of sources. In the early issues of his almanac, Franklin tended to rely on such collections of proverbs as James Howell's *Lexicon Tetraglotton* (1659) and Thomas Fuller's *Gnomologia* (1732). These were not all in a moral vein; as Van Doren has said, Poor Richard's early period was distinctly "gamy." As time went on, however, Franklin turned more often to literary and moralistic aphorisms, which he found in books such as Fuller's *Introductio ad Prudentiam* (1727), Charles Palmer's *Collection of Select Aphorisms and Maxims* (1748), Lord Halifax's *Thoughts and Reflections* (1750), and Samuel Richardson's appendix to *Clarissa* (1751). Other sources were *Wits Recreation* (1654) by John Mennes and James Smith and an anonymous *Collection of Epigrams* (1735–37). For short poems he plundered John Gay's *Fables* (1727–38), Edward Young's *Universal Passion* (1725–28), Pope's *Essay on Man* (1733), and James Savage's *Public Spirit* (1747). Rabelais, Francis Bacon, La Rochefoucauld, John Ray, John Dryden, Matthew Prior, and George Lillo he knew at first or second hand. He was an expert in the literature of the concise and succinct statement. All his life, in fact, he loved to quote proverbial and well-turned phrases. On one occasion he wrote of his own life as an epigram which, although some of its lines were barely tolerable, he hoped to conclude with a bright point.

Franklin's revisions of his borrowed materials, particularly the prose, were sometimes extensive. His admiration for conciseness was perhaps the determining factor, but he experimented with metaphor, occasional rhyme, and of course the familiar rhetorical devices, particularly balance and climax. Van Doren and Charles W. Meister give many examples, of which a few must suffice here.

Franklin's skill in compression is well illustrated by "Fish and visitors smell in three days," thought to derive from John Ray's "Fresh fish and new come guests smell, by that they are three days old." His sharpening of metaphor may be seen in "Neither a fortress nor a maid will hold out long after they begin to parley," from a Scottish proverb, "A listening damsel and a speaking castle shall never end with honor," and by "Time is an herb that cures all diseases," from Lillo's "Time and reflection cure all ills." His fondness for balance may explain the transformation of Fuller's "The fox is grey before he's good" into "Many foxes grow gray, but few grow good." The mastery of climax, or anticlimax, is evident in "Let thy maidservant be faithful, strong, and homely" and "None preaches better than the ant, and she says nothing."

In one extended borrowing, noted by Van Doren, Franklin deliberately Americanized his material. At the end of *Pantagruel* Rabelais has a book on prognostications, with a chapter on eclipses. This year, he says, "Saturn will be retrograde, Venus direct, Mercury as unfix'd as quicksilver. . . . For this reason the crabs will go side-long, and the rope-makers backward . . . bacon will run away from pease in lent; the belly will waddle before; the a—— will sit down first; there won't be a bean left in a twelfth-cake, nor an ace in a flush; the dice won't run as you wish, tho' you cog them, and the chance that you desire will seldom come; brutes shall speak in several places . . . and there will be above twenty and seven irregular verbs made this year, if Priscian doesn't hold them in." In the almanac for 1739 Franklin reworks the passage as follows: "During the first visible Eclipse *Saturn* is retrograde: For which Reason the Crabs will go sidelong, and the Ropemakers backward. The Belly will wag before, and the A—— shall sit down first. *Mercury* will have his share in these Affairs, and so confound the Speech of People, that when a *Pensilvanian* would say PANTHER he shall say PAINTER. When a New Yorker thinks to say (THIS) he shall say (DISS) and the People in *New England* and *Cape-May* will not be

able to say (cow) for their Lives, but will be forc'd to say (KEOW)
by a certain involuntary Twist in the Root of their Tongues. No
Connecticut-Man nor *Marylander* will be able to open his Mouth
this Year, but (SIR) shall be the first or last Syllable he pronounces,
and sometimes both. Brutes shall speak in many Places, and there
will be above seven and twenty irregular Verbs made this Year, if
Grammar don't interpose." Franklin is not at his best here, but his
eye is obviously on his audience and his ear attuned to the vernacu-
lar, as it was in many of Poor Richard's more successful borrowings.

By the time he was thirty, Franklin had a prospering printing
house, a successful newspaper, and a popular almanac. He had too
active a mind, however, to be content with business. Temperamen-
tally disposed toward the improvement of the society of which he
was a part, he looked at the world about him with a critical but op-
timistic eye. His disappointments and his failures he was able to
write off quickly, turning to new projects with undiminished en-
thusiasm. Apathy he appears never to have experienced, and only
rarely was he cynical. These qualities, which account for much of
his personal charm, appear consistently in the writings of his middle
years. For convenience they may be treated under three themes —
promotion, science, and politics.

Because he thought a newspaper should be informative and enter-
taining rather than an instrument for influencing public opinion, he
rarely used the *Pennsylvania Gazette* for promotion. His early
schemes, such as that which resulted in the first American subscrip-
tion library, were urged by word of mouth, and indeed he always
seems to have done some talking before resorting to print. For a
larger audience, however, he turned to the broadside and pamphlet,
the customary promotion devices of his day. The most important
of his promotional tracts is probably *Proposals Relating to the Education of Youth in Pensilvania* (1749). The scheme it proposed had

been in his mind for at least six years, and for once he laid some groundwork for it by reprinting in the *Gazette* a letter from the younger Pliny to Tacitus on the subject of education. His pamphlet, a month later, did not get Franklin what he wanted, but it remains a thought-provoking example of his literary strategy.

What he wanted was an academy with a curriculum better adapted to the needs of Pennsylvania youth than that of the traditional Latin grammar school. He hoped to get it by obtaining the financial support of wealthy citizens, most of whom were conservatives and saw little wrong with the central place of Latin and Greek in the training of young gentlemen. Franklin, who a quarter century earlier had satirized the classical tradition at Harvard College, was convinced that it was time for reform, for a new emphasis upon training in English and in practical subjects.

His preface is therefore designed to conciliate a possibly hostile audience. Some public-spirited gentlemen have already approved the plan; he now puts it into print in order "to obtain the Sentiments and Advice of Men of Learning, Understanding, and Experience in these Matters." With their help it can perhaps be carried into execution. If so, they will have "the hearty Concurrence and Assistance of many who are Wellwishers to their Country." Those who incline "to favour the Design with their Advice, either as to the Parts of Learning to be taught, the Order of Study, the Method of Teaching, the Oeconomy of the School, or any other Matter of Importance to the Success of the Undertaking, are desired to communicate their Sentiments as soon as may be, by Letter directed to *B. Franklin*, Printer, in *Philadelphia*."

The pose of the humble seeker of advice is belied, however, by the pamphlet itself. Before he begins Franklin lists the authors to be quoted: "The famous *Milton*," "the great Mr. *Locke*," "the ingenious Mr. *Hutcheson*" (actually David Fordyce), "the learned Mr. *Obadiah Walker*," "the much admired Mons. *Rollin*," and "the learned and ingenious Dr. *George Turnbull.*" The steel hand beneath the velvet glove is clear: only a vain and provincial Philadelphian will oppose such champions. Then comes the scheme, in which the only concession to the classicists in the actual text is that the rector of the academy should be "learn'd in the Languages and Sciences," a combination which at that date would have required something of a paragon. The crux of the argument (which in differing forms is still with us) lies in seven brief paragraphs:

"As to their STUDIES, it would be well if they could be taught *every Thing* that is useful, and *every Thing* that is ornamental: But Art is long, and their Time is short. It is therefore propos'd that they learn those Things that are likely to be *most useful* and *most ornamental*. Regard being had to the several Professions for which they are intended.

"All should be taught to write a *fair Hand*, and swift, as that is useful to All. And with it may be learnt something of *Drawing*, by Imitation of Prints, and some of the first Principles of Perspective.

"*Arithmetick, Accounts*, and some of the first Principles of *Geometry* and *Astronomy*.

"The *English* Language might be taught by Grammar; in which some of our best Writers, as *Tillotson, Addison, Pope, Algernoon Sidney, Cato's Letters*, &c., should be Classicks; the *Stiles* principally to be cultivated, being the *clear* and the *concise*. Reading should also be taught, and pronouncing, properly, distinctly, emphatically; not with an even Tone, which *under-does*, nor a theatrical, which *over-does* Nature.

"To form their Stile they should be put on Writing Letters to each other, making Abstracts of what they read; or writing the same Things, in their own Words; telling or writing Stories lately read, in their own Expressions. All to be revis'd and corrected by the Tutor, who should give his Reasons, and explain the Force and Import of Words, &c.

"To form their Pronunciation, they may be put on making Declamations, repeating Speeches, delivering Orations, &c., the Tutor assisting at the Rehearsals, teaching, advising, correcting their Accent, &c."

28

Here, in little more than 250 words, is the summation of Franklin's conviction, obviously based upon his own experience and making use of some of the learning processes which he himself had found profitable. That he knew it to be unpopular with his audience is clear from the elaborate support of it by authority. For these 250-odd words he provided more than 3000 words of footnotes, largely direct quotations, with the great Mr. Locke most prominent among those who had argued for training youth in their native language.

The academy was formed, and later a college, with some provisions for instruction such as Franklin wanted. He himself chose the first provost, the Reverend William Smith, a man well disposed toward the sciences. Smith, however, compromised with the classicists and later became Franklin's bitter political enemy. The pose of the humble inquirer and the marshaling of authorities both failed. Franklin did not take that defeat philosophically, and in 1789, the year before his death, charged in his "Observations Relative to the Intentions of the Original Founders of the Academy in Philadelphia" that the English program had been injudiciously starved while favors were showered upon the Latin part. There is in mankind, he said, "an unaccountable prejudice in favor of ancient customs and habitudes, which inclines to a continuance of them after the circumstances, which formerly made them useful, cease to exist." He illustrated the point by a characteristic story of how hats, once generally worn, had been replaced by wigs and umbrellas. Yet, because of fashion, men still carried them under their arms, "though the utility of such a mode . . . is by no means apparent, and it is attended not only with some expense, but with a degree of constant trouble."

The writing which made Franklin world-famous was of course that related to science. Although he was interested in natural phenomena throughout his life, his chief contributions to the knowledge of electricity were made between 1746 and 1752. The subject was fashionable from 1745, when articles on it by William Watson appeared in the *Philosophical Transactions* of the Royal Society of London. Franklin heard some lecture-demonstrations, read Watson's papers, and when a few pieces of apparatus were sent to the Library Company he and some of his friends began to explore electrical phenomena. Their discoveries were reported by Franklin in letters to Peter Collinson, a Quaker merchant of London, who read some of them before the Royal Society and arranged for others to be printed in the *Gentleman's Magazine*. Collinson was also responsible in part for the publication of a collection, *Experiments and Observations on Electricity*, in 1751. Before 1769 four additional English editions, with new letters, had been printed. French translations appeared in 1752 and 1756, a German one in 1758, and an Italian in 1774.

Science brought into play all of Franklin's best qualities as a writer. It demanded clarity and conciseness. The persona of the humble inquirer fitted perfectly, for in science there is little respect for dogmatism. Yet there was room for imagination, since from the phenomena observed hypotheses had to be constructed, and for persuasion, because those hypotheses had to be supported. For once the writer and his audience were in complete accord. Franklin's literary skill is attested by the general acceptance of some of the terms he invented — *positive*, *negative*, *battery*, and *conductor*. His passion for doing good was satisfied, moreover, in his invention of the lightning rod for protecting property from one of the more destructive forces of the natural world.

Many letters in the *Experiments and Observations* are models of reporting and evaluating scientific investigation. The best, perhaps, and certainly the most famous, is the paper proposing the grounded lightning rod (the general theory had been previously stated) and the experimental demonstration of the hypothesis of the identity of electricity and lightning. To illustrate requires a long quotation, but no better example of Franklin's clarity or of the high order of his scientific imagination can readily be found.

After some remarks on the nature of the electrical fluid or element, Franklin notes that the charge in an electrified body can be drawn off by the point of a pin from a foot's distance, while if the head of the pin is the attracting agent it must be moved to within a few inches of the electrified body before a charge is drawn off. Points apparently draw off the electrical atmosphere more readily than blunt bodies do; "as in the plucking the hairs from the horse's tail, a degree of strength insufficient to pull away a handful at once, could yet easily strip it hair by hair; so a blunt body presented cannot draw off a number of particles at once; but a pointed one, with no greater force, takes them away easily, particle by particle." Franklin is not sure of the true reasons for this phenomenon, but it is not of much importance, he says, "to know the manner in which nature exercises her laws; 'tis enough if we know the laws themselves. 'Tis of real use to know, that china left in the air unsupported will fall and break; but *how* it comes to fall, and *why* it breaks, are matters of speculation. 'Tis a pleasure indeed to know them, but we can preserve our china without it." He goes on:

"Thus in the present case, to know this power of points, may possibly be of some use to mankind, tho' we should never be able to explain it. The following experiments . . . show this power. I have a large prime conductor made of several thin sheets of Fuller's pasteboard form'd into a tube, near 10 feet long and a foot diameter. It is covered with *Dutch* emboss'd paper, almost totally gilt. This large metallic surface supports a much greater electrical atmosphere than a rod of iron of 50 times the weight would do. It is suspended by silk lines, and when charg'd will strike at near two inches distance, a pretty hard stroke so as to make ones knuckle ach. Let a person standing on the floor present the point of a needle, at 12 or more inches distance from it, and while the needle is so presented, the conductor cannot be charged, the point drawing off the fire as fast as it is thrown on by the electrical globe. Let it be charged, and then present the point at the same distance, and it will suddenly be discharged. In the dark you may see a light on the point, when the experiment is made. And if the person holding the point stands upon wax, he will be electrified by receiving the fire at that distance. Attempt to draw off the electricity with a blunt body, as a bolt of iron round at the end and smooth (a silversmith's iron punch, inch-thick, is what I use) and you must bring it within the distance of three inches before you can do it, and then it is done with a stroke and crack. As the pasteboard tube hangs loose on silk lines, when you approach it with the punch iron, it likewise will move towards the punch, being attracted while it is charged; but if at the same instant a point be presented as before, it retires again, for the point discharges it. Take a pair of large brass scales, of two or more feet beam, the cords of the scales being silk. Suspend the beam by a packthread from the cieling, so that the bottom of the scales may be about a foot from the floor: the scales will move round in a circle by the untwisting of the packthread. Set the iron punch on the end upon the floor, in such a place as that the scales may pass over it in making their circle: Then electrify one scale by applying the wire of a charged phial to it. As they move round, you see that scale draw nigher to the floor, and dip more when it comes over the punch; and if that be placed at a proper distance, the scale will snap and discharge its fire into it. But if a needle be stuck on the end of the punch, its point upwards, the scale, instead of drawing nigh to the punch and snapping, discharges its fire silently, through the point, and rises higher from the punch. Nay, even if the needle be placed upon the floor, near the punch, its point upwards, the end of the punch, tho' so much higher than the needle, will not attract the scale and receive its fire, for the needle will get it and convey it away, before it comes nigh enough for the punch to act. And this is constantly observable in these experiments, that the greater quantity of electricity on the pasteboard tube, the farther it strikes or discharges its fire, and the point likewise will draw it off at a still greater distance.

"Now if the fire of electricity and that of lightening be the same . . . this pasteboard tube and these scales may represent electrified clouds. If a tube of only 10 feet long will strike and discharge its fire on the punch at two or three inches distance, an electrified cloud of perhaps 10,000 acres may strike and discharge on the earth at a proportionably greater distance. The horizontal motion of the scales over the floor, may represent the motion of the clouds over the earth; and the erect iron punch a hill or high building; and then we see how electrified clouds passing over hills or high buildings at too great a height to strike, may be attracted lower till within their striking distance. And lastly, if a needle fix'd on the punch with its point upright, or even on the floor, below the punch, will draw the fire from the scale silently at a much greater than the striking distance, and so prevent its descending towards the punch; or if in its course it would have come nigh enough to strike, yet being first deprived of its fire it cannot, and the punch is thereby secured from the stroke. I say, if these things are so, may not the knowledge of this power of points be of use to mankind, in preserving houses, churches, ships &c. from the stroke of lightning, by directing us to fix on the highest parts of those edifices, upright rods of iron, made sharp as a needle, and gilt to prevent rusting, and from the foot of these rods a wire down the outside of the building into the ground; or down round one of the shrouds of a ship and down her side till it reaches the water? Would not these pointed rods probably draw the electrical fire silently out of a cloud before it came nigh enough to strike, and thereby secure us from the most sudden and terrible mischief?

"To determine the question, whether the clouds that contain lightning are electrified or not, I would propose an experiment to be try'd where it may be done conveniently. On the top of some high tower or steeple, place a kind of sentry-box . . . big enough to contain a man and an electrical stand. From the middle of the stand let an iron rod rise and pass bending out of the door, and then upright 20 or 30 feet, pointed very sharp at the end. If the electrical stand be kept clean and dry, a man standing on it when such clouds are passing low, might be electrified and afford sparks, the rod drawing fire to him from a cloud. If any danger to the man should be apprehended (tho' I think there would be none) let him stand on the floor of his box, and now and then bring near to the rod, the loop of a wire that has one end fastened to the leads, he holding it by a wax handle; so the sparks, if the rod is electrified, will strike from the rod to the wire, and not affect him."

Franklin constructs his hypothesis, with its usefulness firmly in mind, from careful observation of experiments with simple apparatus easily obtainable by anyone. His description is clear and factual, although the analogies of the horse's tail and the falling china are valuable aids to understanding. His conclusions are the earliest written suggestions of their kind, and they quickly came to fruition. Lightning rods were erected and found to work, and on May 13, 1752, Thomas-François Dalibard reported to the Academy of Sciences in Paris on his successful performance of the proposed experiment with a tall pointed rod and an electrical stand. "En suivant la route que M. Franklin nous a tracée," he began, "j'ai obtenu une satisfaction complète." With that sentence the triumph of Franklin the natural philosopher was assured. It was to be some weeks before he was to fly his famous kite, in a simpler but much more dangerous experiment.

Franklin's first skirmish with power politics on the international level, where the ravages of war as a means of settling conflicts of interest are an ever-present risk, came at about the same time that he was beginning his exploration of electricity, in 1747. England had been at war with Spain since 1739 and with France since 1740, which meant that the British colonies had enemies to the south in the Spanish Main and to the north in French Canada. To the west, moreover, were the Indians, with whom the French could make alliances. If English sea power failed, the colonies would be encircled. It took some time for this fact to disturb Pennsylvanians. Their geographical location seemed to promise safety; the powerful Quaker leaders were conscientiously opposed to all things military, including preparation against attack; and the numerous German farmers and artisans cared nothing for British supremacy. Then, in the spring and summer of 1747, Spanish and French privateers appeared in the Delaware River, one of them raiding a settlement less than sixty miles from Philadelphia. The War of the Austrian Succession was suddenly something that had to be reckoned with.

Franklin's *Plain Truth: Or, Serious Considerations on the Present State of the City of Philadelphia, and Province of Pennsylvania,* which appeared in November, is his most effective piece of propaganda. Its purpose was to arouse a divided community to the desperate necessity of unity and action. Like Thomas Paine's *Common Sense* it is an appeal to emotion rather than to reason, directed to almost every special interest which might suffer if the worst should happen and the city and province be attacked. Like Paine, too, Franklin offered a specific course of action, one quickly followed.

Plain Truth has upon its title page a long Latin quotation from Cato, not for ornament but to satisfy the learned that military preparedness had classical precedent. Its first paragraph ends with a proverb, "When the Steed is stolen, you shut the Stable Door," a warning the most illiterate could understand. Every other British colony has taken measures for its defense, Franklin notes. The wealth of Pennsylvania, unprotected, must certainly be a temptation to an enemy which has been exploring the river approaches, is known to have spies everywhere, and very probably has subverted unscrupulous men within the province itself. Remember, Franklin says, the eighth chapter of Judges, which he quotes at length. The French Catholics have converted many Indians, and it may not be long before the scalping parties which have already raided New York will be ravaging the back country of Pennsylvania. City and country are alike in being threatened, and their interests are the same. Trade is in dire danger, and if trade declines bad debts will multiply and land values decrease. The enemy may count upon Quaker pacifism, although Franklin thinks some Quakers will fight in self-defense. Preparedness will cost money, but think of the loss from plundering and burning. Well-to-do Philadelphians may be granted time to flee to the country, but what if there is a sudden attack, "perhaps in the Night! Confined to your Houses, you will have nothing to trust to but the Enemy's Mercy. Your best Fortune will be, to fall under the Power of Commanders of King's Ships, able to controul the Mariners; and not into the Hands of *licentious Privateers*. Who can, without the utmost Horror, conceive the Miseries of the Latter! when your Persons, Fortunes, Wives and Daughters, shall be subject to the wanton and unbridled Rage, Rapine, and Lust, of *Negroes*, *Molattoes*, and others, the vilest and most abandoned of Mankind." The governing party, not even "Friends" to the people (he is here playing on the formal name for the Quakers), will not permit the appropriation of the funds necessary for defense, nor is anything to be hoped for from the opposition, who will not lay out their wealth to protect the trade of their Quaker adversaries. " 'Till of late I could scarce believe the Story of him who refused to pump in a sinking Ship, because one on board, whom he hated, would be saved by it as well as himself. But such, it seems, is the Unhappiness of human Nature, that our Passions, when violent, often are too hard for the united Force of *Reason*, *Duty*, and *Religion*." What must be done, therefore, will have to be done by the "middling People"—farmers, shopkeepers, and tradesmen. They are strong enough to muster 60,000 men, exclusive of the Quakers, and all of them are acquainted with the use of firearms. Englishmen have shown before that they can fight, and there are thousands of "*brave* and *steady*" Germans. If the hints of the author, "A Tradesman of Philadelphia," are well received, he will within a few days lay before the people the form of an association, "together with a practicable Scheme for raising the Money necessary for the Defence of our Trade, City, and Country, without laying a Burthen on any Man." The tract then concludes with a prayer.

Here Franklin addressed himself to selfish interests, fear, and prejudice—national, social, racial, and religious. The humble inquirer is forgotten, together with caution other than that which might conciliate the more militant Quakers. *Plain Truth* made him enemies in high places, chief among them Thomas Penn, the proprietor, but it got results. The extralegal association for defense which he proposed was organized almost immediately, despite the objection that it constituted a private army which might be a potential source of danger to government. The money was raised by a lottery which Franklin showed the "middling" people how to run. Arms were procured and the province readied for a battle which fortunately never came, the exhausted great powers of Europe signing the Treaty of Aix-la-Chapelle in 1748. The association thereafter languished, but Franklin was now a man of political influence. He exerted himself again in large affairs in 1754, during the Albany Congress, at which he proposed a plan of colonial union and editorialized in the *Gazette* for that cause, printing the first American newspaper cartoon: a segmented snake, representing the several colonies, above a caption reading "Join, or die." He also took a leading part in the American phase of the Seven Years' War, but never again did he display the sustained passion of the propagandist which *Plain Truth* reveals.

During his two long stays in London Franklin's tasks were essentially diplomatic. His first assignment was to get some settlement of a dispute about taxes which had soured the relations between the Pennsylvania assembly and the Penn family, who retained immense proprietary rights in provincial lands. Later his job was to represent the colonial interests to the British ministry, increasingly hostile as its measures for taxation were opposed by the Americans, and to the British public, which tended to be indifferent to issues so remote. Because of these responsibilities, Franklin's writing between 1757 and 1775 was predominantly political, although he did not neglect science and occasionally found time for such *jeux d'esprits* as the

"Craven Street Gazette" of 1770, a fictitious newspaper prepared for the Stevenson family, with whom he lodged for many years.

Over 125 anonymous contributions to English newspapers between 1765 and 1775 have been identified as Franklin's. In addition he had a hand in a number of important pamphlets and sometimes appeared in public to testify, as an expert witness, on American opinion. Facing a hostile or apathetic audience, he was usually ingratiating and conciliatory, appealing to the British concern for national interests and fair play. Only at the end did he despair of settling the quarrel without separation and bloodshed.

Of his pamphlets the most considerable was *The Interest of Great Britain Considered, with Regard to Her Colonies and the Acquisition of Canada and Guadaloupe* (1760). Written toward the end of the Seven Years' War, it strongly urged the annexation of Canada as a condition of peace. Strange as it may now seem, there were some Englishmen who preferred to acquire Guadaloupe, an island group in the West Indies where sugar was already being produced in large quantity. One of their arguments for leaving Canada to the French was that British America was already large enough, since if it grew stronger it might become dangerous to Great Britain. In preparing his answer to this line of reasoning Franklin had the help of an English lawyer-friend, Richard Jackson, and the tone of the piece is largely legalistic. Here and there, however, Franklin's feelings enliven things, as in his suggestion that the growth of the colonies could be checked less cruelly if Parliament should emulate the Egyptian treatment of the Israelites and pass a law requiring midwives to stifle every third or fourth child at birth.

In February 1766, Franklin appeared before the House of Commons in the course of a debate on the repeal of the Stamp Act. He made an impressive showing, not that he was an accomplished orator but because of his talent as a face-to-face persuader. His answers to questions, stenographically reported, reveal a well-planned strategy for dealing with an audience partly friendly and partly hostile. Usually he replied in a sentence or two, but he added more when he saw the chance to appeal to British self-interest or patriotism, and on three or four occasions he spoke at length. Again and again he stood firm on the main point, that the colonies were right in their distinction between external taxes, properly levied for the regulation of commerce, and internal taxes, which they insisted should be imposed only by their own legislatures.

Typical of the many newspaper contributions is "The Causes of American Discontents before 1768," an even-tempered explanation of colonial grievances as they might appear to a disinterested Englishman. In this and many other letters Franklin's role was to inform rather than to argue; he was what we would now call a public relations man. By 1773, however, he was understandably discouraged, and his two best known newspaper articles are satires: "Rules by Which a Great Empire May Be Reduced to a Small One" and "An Edict by the King of Prussia." He himself said they were "designed to expose the conduct of this country towards the colonies in a short, comprehensive, and striking view, and stated therefore in out-of-the-way forms, as most likely to take the general attention."

The "Rules," one of his most ironic pieces, indirectly but clearly suggests rebellion, and reviews American complaints in highly emotional language. One paragraph will illustrate its method and feeling: "However peaceably your colonies have submitted to your government, shown their affection to your interests, and patiently borne their grievances; you are to suppose them *always inclined to revolt*, and treat them accordingly. Quarter troops among them, who by their insolence may provoke the rising of mobs, and by their bullets and bayonets suppress them. By this means, like the husband who uses his wife ill from suspicion, you may in time convert your suspicions into realities."

The "Edict" is the most effective of what Paul Baender has called

Franklin's "duplicative" satires, in which the strategy was to demand that the reader put himself in someone else's place, so that he may feel more keenly feelings which he might otherwise misunderstand. It is also a hoax, whose success greatly pleased its joke-loving author. What Franklin did was to use the very words of the Parliamentary statutes restricting American commerce and manufactures, ranging from the reign of Charles II to that of George III, as if they were enacted by Prussia, a nation with some claim to being Britain's mother country from the time of the Angles and the Saxons. The "Edict" makes clearer than any lengthy argument how shipping and manufacturing interests had "lobbied" for their own advantage over the shipowners, ironmakers, and hatters of the colonies. But by this time, no literary skill could long postpone the appeal to arms.

Having failed to avert the rebellion he dreaded, Franklin returned to Philadelphia long enough to serve on the committee which drafted the Declaration of Independence. By the end of 1776, however, he was back in Europe, this time in Paris, to plead the cause of a new nation and to deal with still another public, this time a most admiring one.

One of his first acts, apparently, was to compose still another hoax. "The Sale of the Hessians" attacks the British employment of German mercenaries in the American war. It is a letter in French, ostensibly written in Rome by the Count de Schaumbergh, to the commander of the German soldiers for whose services the British were paying large subsidies, including lump sums for men killed. Nearly 30,000 Germans were thus hired out by their princes, and in one case the agreement was to count three wounded men as one dead one in reckoning up the account. Franklin's matter-of-fact assumption of the Count's desire to have as many casualties as possible leads to cutting irony.

"I am about to send to you some new recruits. Don't economize them. Remember glory before all things. Glory is true wealth.

There is nothing degrades the soldier like the love of money. He must care only for honour and reputation, but this reputation must be acquired in the midst of dangers. A battle gained without costing the conqueror any blood is an inglorious success, while the conquered cover themselves with glory by perishing with their arms in their hands. Do you remember that of the 300 Lacedæmonians who defended the defile of Thermopylæ, not one returned? How happy should I be could I say the same of my brave Hessians!

"It is true that their king, Leonidas, perished with them: but things have changed, and it is no longer the custom for princes of the empire to go and fight in America for a cause with which they have no concern. And besides, to whom should they pay the thirty guineas per man if I did not stay in Europe to receive them? Then, it is necessary also that I be ready to send recruits to replace the men you lose. For this purpose I must return to Hesse. It is true, grown men are becoming scarce there, but I will send you boys. Besides, the scarcer the commodity the higher the price. I am assured that the women and little girls have begun to till our lands, and they get on not badly. You did right to send back to Europe that Dr. Crumerus who was so successful in curing dysentery. Don't bother with a man who is subject to looseness of the bowels. That disease makes bad soldiers. One coward will do more mischief in an engagement than ten brave men will do good. Better that they burst in their barracks than fly in a battle, and tarnish the glory of our arms. Besides, you know that they pay me as killed for all who die from disease, and I don't get a farthing for runaways."

Franklin's busy life in France, where he received the adulation usually reserved for matinee idols, was not all grimly political. Living at Passy, then a Paris suburb, he became the center of a group of admirers, many of them women. For their amusement and his own he set up a printing press in his house, upon which were printed, from time to time, short light essays, of a sort sometimes known as *bijoux*. These are usually referred to as the "bagatelles," and there are nineteen of them altogether. The best known are "Dialogue between Franklin and the Gout," "The Whistle," "The Ephemera," and "The Morals of Chess." All exploit an old man's personality or hobbies and, since they were written for a French audience, they have an unusual flavor for English writing — a Gallic delight in the well-turned phrase and the expression of delicate feeling. They are carefully structured, with the tone sustained just long enough for their effect. There is some moralizing, to be sure; that had become a habit of Franklin's.

Every reader has his favorite bagatelle, and few fail to be charmed by one of them or another. My favorite is "The Ephemera," addressed to Madame Brillon, a woman many years Franklin's junior whom he called by the pet name of "Brillante." It is an allegory, "an emblem of human life," which compares men and women to a species of small flies. One white-haired philosopher fly, seven hours old, reflects upon his lot, now that he cannot hope to live more than seven or eight minutes longer. What to him are politics, or scientific investigations, or a name to leave behind him? "For me," he concludes, "after all my eager pursuits, no solid pleasures now remain, but the reflection of a long life spent in meaning well, the sensible conversations of a few good lady ephemeræ, and now and then a kind smile and a tune from the ever amiable *Brillante*." In that gallant commentary on fame and old age Franklin comes alive more fully than he ever does in the *Autobiography*.

Autobiography is, indeed, an imperfect instrument at best. Memory, whether conscious or unconscious, is tricky and mysterious, and a biographer is sometimes able to get the facts more accurately than he who seeks to explain himself. What the autobiographer does not tell us is sometimes more significant than what he does.

Franklin's autobiography, for example, omits consideration of a vast area of his early life which must have had important psychological effects. He recounts some of his sexual adventures and admits that in his first years in Philadelphia he was resorting to "low

Women" to allay "that hard-to-be-govern'd Passion of Youth," but he does not say that a son was born to him in the winter of 1730–31 by a woman who has never been satisfactorily identified. She may have been Deborah Read, whom he took as his common-law wife in September of 1730, regular marriage being impossible because her runaway husband might still have been alive. Deborah was his faithful companion until her death in 1774, but of their life together we know little other than that she brought up William, the illegitimate son, as well as their daughter Sarah, and that she did not have the capacity to share the intellectual growth and social success of her printer husband. It is hard to escape the conviction that the Franklins were always on the wrong side of the tracks, and that some of Benjamin's pleasures in his diplomatic triumphs (he was, some have thought, a bit of a snob in later life) may be explained by his domestic situation.

The *Autobiography* was begun as a letter to William, who had already given Franklin an illegitimate grandson, and for whom some moralizing was no doubt appropriate. (William was later, as the last royal governor of New Jersey, to break with his father over politics.) Franklin wrote eighty-six pages of it in England in 1771; other parts were added later (seventeen pages in 1784 and 117 pages in 1788, all written in France, and a final seven and a half pages in 1790, in Philadelphia). Its piecemeal composition was followed by piecemeal publication, in which Franklin of course had no hand, so that until very recently no reliable text has been available. These circumstances, together with its coverage of only the first part of Franklin's life, make it a remarkably imperfect book.

One much-discussed question about the *Autobiography* has been its style. In the late nineteenth century it was believed that Temple Franklin, editor of the first "official" version in 1818, had systematically substituted Latin words for his grandfather's more vigorous

Anglo-Saxon expressions. He was accused of changing "guzzlers of beer" to "drinkers of beer," "Keimer stared like a pig poisoned" to "Keimer stared with astonishment," and making other similar concessions to false gentility. Max Farrand's lengthy examination of the original manuscript, however, has shown that many changes of this kind were probably Franklin's own. In the last months of his life he was apparently much less admiring of a colloquial style than he was in 1771. He seems, indeed, to have grown conservative about language as he grew older, expressing opposition to innovations which he feared might hamper communication between Englishmen and Americans. One wonders what would have been the result had he lived to see the *Autobiography* through the press himself. Or, what is even more frightening, had he edited his own collected works.

For these and various other reasons Franklin is probably best and most fully revealed in those writings with which he had no opportunity to tamper, and particularly in his letters. Of these there are hundreds, to his family (including a lively and favorite sister in Boston, Mrs. Jane Mecom), to his scientific and philosophical friends, and to correspondents who, like Ezra Stiles, invaded his privacy with a slight touch of malice. The majority of his letters date from the latter part of his life. They show his warm feelings for his friends, which were ordinarily warmly reciprocated, the extraordinary range of his interests, and the play of a lively and imaginative mind. That he had a long life of "meaning well" is clear enough.

It should be evident by this time that I believe Franklin was right in thinking of himself as a writer and that he was seldom as calculating and unemotional a writer as he thought he was. He had a purpose in almost everything he wrote, usually persuasion. He believed written persuasion to be distinct from oral, and he always came back to clarity, brevity, and purpose. An essay of 1733, discovered by Whitfield J. Bell, Jr., contains a passage which sums up his conception of

44

the difference between writing and speech. "*Amplification*, or the Art of saying Little in Much," it reads,

"should only be allowed to Speakers. If they preach, a Discourse of considerable Length is expected from them, upon every Subject they undertake, and perhaps they are not stock'd with naked Thought sufficient to furnish it out. If they plead in the Courts, it is of Use to speak abundance, tho' they reason little; for the Ignorant in a Jury, can scarcely believe it possible that a Man can talk so much and so long without being in the Right. Let them have the Liberty then, of repeating the same Sentences in other Words; let them put an Adjective to every Substantive, and double every Substantive with a Synonima; for this is more agreeable than hauking, spitting, taking Snuff, or any other Means of concealing Hesitation. Let them multiply Definitions, Comparisons, Similitudes and Examples. Permit them to make a Detail of Causes and Effects, enumerate all the Consequences, and express one Half by Metaphor and Circumlocution: Nay, allow the Preacher to tell us whatever a Thing is negatively, before he begins to tell us what it is affirmatively; and suffer him to divide and subdivide as far as *Two and fiftieth*. All this is not intolerable while it is not written. But when a Discourse is to be bound down upon Paper, and subjected to the calm leisurely Examination of nice Judgment, every Thing that is needless gives Offence; and therefore all should be retrenched, that does not directly conduce to the End design'd."

The final judgment upon the question of whether or not Franklin was a great writer rests upon the evaluation of his purposes. If the advancement of science and the resolution of political differences are of major importance, he was. If the exploration of the depths of human psychology is the primary purpose of literature, he was not. If the great thing for the writer to do is to present a thought-provoking or satisfying philosophy of life, the question is debatable. Purpose aside, however, and greatness left to individual opinion, Franklin has one telling advantage over most American writers who must be read in the context of their time. People do read him.

⤳ Selected Bibliography

Collected Works of Benjamin Franklin

The Works of Benjamin Franklin, edited by Jared Sparks. 10 vols., Boston: Hilliard, Gray and Co., 1840.

The Writings of Benjamin Franklin, edited by Albert Henry Smyth. 10 vols., New York: Macmillan, 1905–7.

The Papers of Benjamin Franklin, edited by Leonard Labaree and others. 4 vols. to date (January 6, 1706, to June 30, 1753). New Haven: Yale University Press, 1959–61. (A joint project of the Yale University Press and the American Philosophical Society, expected to run to 24 vols. when completed.)

Principal Separate Works and Periodical Publications

FRANKLIN wrote only a few books. Many of his best known pieces were circulated in manuscript; others were printed anonymously and without title in newspapers. The following list is selective, with emphasis on items available in modern or facsimile editions. Those marked with an asterisk were originally untitled; a dagger indicates anonymous publication.

*† The Silence Dogood Papers, *New England Courant*, April 2–October 8, 1722.

† *A Dissertation on Liberty and Necessity, Pleasure and Pain.* London: n.p., 1725. Edited in facsimile by Lawrence C. Wroth, New York: Facsimile Text Society, 1930.

† *A Modest Enquiry into the Nature and Necessity of a Paper-Currency.* Philadelphia: n.p., 1729.

Poor Richard, 1733. An Almanack for the Year of Christ 1733. Philadelphia: B. Franklin, [1732]. (First of twenty-five annual issues for which Franklin prepared the literary content. There are many selective reprints, such as *Poor Richard's Almanack*, with a Foreword by Phillips Russell (Garden City, N.Y.: Doubleday, Doran, 1928), which prints the 1733, 1749, 1756, 1757, and 1758 issues in facsimile.)

† *Plain Truth: Or, Serious Considerations on the Present State of the City of Philadelphia, and Province of Pennsylvania.* N.p., 1747.

† *Proposals Relating to the Education of Youth in Pensilvania.* N.p., 1749. Edited in facsimile by Randolph G. Adams, Ann Arbor, Mich.: William L.

46

Clements Library, 1927, and by William Pepper, Philadelphia: University of Pennsylvania Press, 1931.

Experiments and Observations on Electricity. London: E. Cave, 1751. (Later editions in 1754, 1760, and 1769. Translations into French (1752 and 1756), German (1758), and Italian (1774).) Edited by I. Bernard Cohen, Cambridge, Mass.: Harvard University Press, 1941.

* Father Abraham's Speech, or "The Way to Wealth," or "Bonhomme Richard," *Poor Richard Improved: Being an Almanack . . . For the Year of Our Lord 1758.* Philadelphia: Franklin and Hall, [1757]. (Separately printed, it is known in more than 150 editions.)

† *The Interest of Great Britain Considered, with Regard to Her Colonies and the Acquisition of Canada and Guadaloupe.* London: T. Becket, 1760. (The best example of a large body of material on British colonial policies; cf. Verner W. Crane, ed., *Benjamin Franklin's Letters to the Press, 1758–1775* (Chapel Hill: University of North Carolina Press, for the Institute of Early American History and Culture, 1950).)

The Examination of Doctor Benjamin Franklin. N.p., n.d. [London: J. Almon, 1766?]

*† The Causes of American Discontents before 1768, *London Chronicle*, January 7, 1768.

† Rules by Which a Great Empire May Be Reduced to a Small One, *Public Advertiser* (London), September 1773.

† An Edict by the King of Prussia, *Public Advertiser*, September 1773.

* Bagatelles. Passy: privately printed, 1779–84? (Most of them are extant in their original form only in a unique volume in the Yale University Library. See Richard E. Amacher, *Franklin's Wit & Folly: The Bagatelles* (New Brunswick, N.J.: Rutgers University Press, 1953).)

Memoires de la vie privée de Benjamin Franklin, écrits par lui-même. Paris: Chez Buisson, 1791. (First printing of the first part of the *Autobiography.* For the intricate history of that work's writing and publication, see *Benjamin Franklin's Memoirs*, Parallel Text Edition edited by Max Farrand (Berkeley and Los Angeles: University of California Press, 1949).)

Current American Reprints

Autobiography. New York: Harper's Modern Classics. $1.40. New York: Dolphin (Doubleday). $.95. New York: Washington Square Press. $.45.

Autobiography and Other Writings (the titles vary). Edited by Henry Steele Commager, New York: Modern Library (Random House). $.65. Edited by Herbert W. Schneider, New York: Liberal Arts (Bobbs-Merrill). $.90. Edited by Dixon Wecter and Larzer Ziff, New York: Rinehart Editions (Holt, Rinehart, Winston). $.75. Edited by Russel B. Nye (text based on Farrand),

Boston: Riverside (Houghton Mifflin). $.75. Edited by L. Jesse Lemisch, New York: Signet Classics (New American Library). $.50.
The Benjamin Franklin Sampler. New York: Premier (Fawcett Publications). $.35.

Bibliography

Ford, Paul Leicester. *Franklin Bibliography: A List of Books Written by, or Relating to Benjamin Franklin.* Brooklyn, N.Y.: Privately printed, 1889.

Spiller, Robert E., and others, eds. *Literary History of the United States.* 3 vols., New York: Macmillan, 1948. (The selective bibliography, III, 507–15, was compiled by Thomas H. Johnson.) *Bibliography Supplement*, edited by Richard M. Ludwig, 1959.

Biographical and Critical Studies

Aldridge, Alfred Owen. *Franklin and His French Contemporaries.* New York: New York University Press, 1957.

Cook, Elizabeth Christine. *Literary Influences in Colonial Newspapers, 1704–1750*, Columbia University Studies in English and Comparative Literature. New York, 1912.

Crane, Verner W. *Benjamin Franklin and a Rising People.* Boston: Little, Brown, 1954.

MacLaurin, Lois Margaret. *Franklin's Vocabulary.* Garden City, N.Y.: Doubleday, Doran, 1928.

McMaster, John Bach. *Benjamin Franklin as a Man of Letters* (American Men of Letters Series). Boston: Houghton, 1887.

Van Doren, Carl. *Benjamin Franklin.* New York: Viking, 1938.

Articles Relating to Franklin as a Writer

Baender, Paul. "The Basis of Franklin's Duplicative Satires," *American Literature*, 32:267–79 (November 1960).

Davy, Francis X. "Benjamin Franklin Satirist: The Satire of Franklin and Its Rhetoric," *Dissertation Abstracts*, 19:317 (1958).

Horner, George F. "Franklin's *Dogood Papers* Reexamined," *Studies in Philology*, 37:501–23 (July 1940).

Meister, Charles W. "Franklin as a Proverb Stylist," *American Literature*, 24:157–66 (May 1952).

Newcomb, Robert. "The Sources of Benjamin Franklin's Sayings of Poor Richard," *Dissertation Abstracts*, 17:2584–85 (1957).

Ross, John F. "The Character of Poor Richard: Its Source and Alteration," *Publications of the Modern Language Association*, 35:785–94 (September 1940).